The Consultant

Direction artistique : Jamie Keenan
Mise en page : MCP
Photo couverture : Marcelo Santos/Getty Images

Enregistrements, montage et mixage : Studio Corby
Texte lu par Saul Jephcott

Dépôt Légal : 6861/01
Achevé d'imprimer par EMD S.A.S. en Juin 2010
N° d'impression : 23252

The Consultant

Rupert Morgan

didier

Day 1

WE ARE CANNIBALS in Dolce & Gabanna, my colleagues and I.

That is what we do at Amelyosis: we eat up other humans as if we were foxes and they were chickens. It's a pretty good job.

That, in any case, is what I found myself thinking this afternoon as I listened to our Chief Executive, Rueben Cicero, welcome us to this tropical island where we have come for a week of intensive management training:

"Amelyosis is not an ordinary business, people!" Cicero shouted as we stood on the sand, our baggage at our feet. He was on a wooden terrace overlooking the beach as he gave his oration:

"Kellogs is a business. Coca-Cola is a business. General Motors is a business. Or... maybe not General Motors, actually."

He paused as we laughed at the sorry condition of the company that had once been the jewel of American consumer culture: a company so influential that whole cities and the landscape itself had been remodelled in accordance with its product. A company that we at Amelyosis helped to 'restructure' last year, axing 45,000 jobs and three factories. They paid us millions to do it. Or, rather, the tax-payers did. Which means, when you think about it, that the very people whose jobs we axed paid us to do it. It's a strange world we humans have invented, isn't it?

Amelyosis is doing well in the recession because it's our job to tell other businesses what they are doing wrong. Good times or bad – it makes no difference to companies like ours. We used to be called Hackersakt Corporate Solutions, but we rebranded ourselves a few years ago. The old name was too 20th Century.

"Why are these businesses really any different to the farmers of old?" he asked rhetorically, "They produce things, they take them to the market, they sell them and make a little profit. Some are selling carrots and some are selling cars – but is there any fundamental difference? It's positively medieval! They are all... *peasants!*"

His eyes blazed with passionate intensity:

"The laws of Nature do not change! The world never changes! Democracy is a beautiful, intricate charade but, at heart, we at Amelyosis know that society is still feudal because that is the *natural* order of things: the strong dominate the weak."

He paused to look at us, a hundred and fifty of Amelyosis's best management consultants. He raised his arms, opening his hands wide as if to hold us in his embrace:

"Amelyosis Corporate Solutions is not a business, my friends. We do not *make* anything. We do not *invent* anything. We do not *sell* anything. So why do corporations pay us hundreds of millions of dollars in consultancy fees each year? Because their managers are *terrified*, that is why. They look at General Motors and think 'Are we next? Will we be conquered by stronger foreign competitors?'. So, just as medieval serfs turned to the Baron and his knights for security, they look to us: Amelyosis!"

I looked around at my colleagues and could see by their expressions that Cicero was pushing all the right buttons. They were loving it.

"We are an elite combat force! We are a warrior tribe! We are Amelyosis! What are we?"

"*Amelyosis!*" came the answer from all around me.

"Who are the strongest?"

"*Amelyosis!*"

I opened my mouth, but no sound came out. This is a little strange, I thought. We are on a beach on a tropical island in the middle of the Indian Ocean, all in expensive designer suits, having a mini-version of the fucking Nuremberg rallies. My colleagues had started a rhythmic chant now, their arms punching the air:

"*Am-el-y-o-sis! Am-el-y-o-sis!*"

I raised my arm, pretending to join in, and looked around me. To my relief, I saw one other person who wasn't chanting. She didn't even have her arm in the air. I didn't know her – there were consultants from different Amelyosis offices all over the world here – but she was attractive, her dark hair cut into a boyish crop, her olive skin suggesting she was from somewhere in southern Europe.

She looked my way and saw that I wasn't chanting along with the others. She smiled and rolled her eyes at me before looking back toward Cicero. I felt my arm slowly drop to my side. Game over.

She came. She saw. She conquered.

Day 2

I

"THIS IS A SAMSON BUG." our guide announced this morning, holding up a particularly ugly specimen of the insect kingdom. He'd taken a group of fifteen of us into the island's jungle interior to learn essential survival skills.

How the company he represents, Optimum Training, thinks this will be useful to us in our capacity as Management Consultants, I do not know. If ever a client of mine back in London asks me to demonstrate how to make fire with two sticks, then I will be able to do it. But I would suggest that his entire business model needs rethinking.

The bug was big, fat and white.

"It's not pretty, but it's packed with protein," the man from Optimum Training said. "Here – breakfast!"

He proffered it to me, apparently wanting me to try this culinary novelty. I looked at it slowly wriggling in the palm of my hand, a sense of nausea in my stomach.

"You have to be joking." I said, "It looks like Jabba the Hutt."

"There are tribes in Papua New Guinea who eat Samson Bugs as a central part of their diet," the guide assured me.

"Because they don't have *Frosties* in Papua New Guinea." I pointed out, "The entire Papuan culture might be different if they'd had the choice of *not* eating little Jabbas for breakfast."

"Come on, James, are you man or mouse?" challenged Nick Sark, a colleague of mine from the London office. "We're in the jungle, not a damned Holiday Inn. If the Papuan pygmies eat them..."

"Then that might explain why they're so fucking *small!*" I interrupted.

I saw Nick's eyes narrow almost imperceptibly, and realised that I should not have denigrated the Papuans for being small. Nick was many things: clever, energetic, ambitious... but the gods had not been generous to him in terms of longitude. I think it was this that motivated him, making him so hungry for success. He had a sense of deep injustice, like a man holding a fork in a world of soup.

"Oh... give it to me, Barbie," he said, snatching the Samson Bug from my hand and putting it into his mouth.

"Actually–" the guide began to say, but it was too late: there was an audible *'pop!'* as Nick's teeth closed on the bug. "–I was only joking. They don't *really* eat them in Papua New Guinea."

The rest of the team and I groaned in disgust, and Nick's eyes opened wide. He nodded his head up and down a few times, and then spat the empty sac of the Samson Bug at the guide's feet.

"*Never* make fun of the people of Papua New Guinea!" he shouted at him in fury, "What are you: a racist?"

"Don't worry: Samson Bugs *are* edible." the guide defended himself, "Just really, really... vile."

II

"B2B or not B2B, that is the question!" Rueben Cicero proclaimed with a passion that suggested a sense of deep personal conviction. Conviction of *what*, exactly, I did not know. So far I had not understood a single thing he'd said. "I see a future world in which proactive, multifunctional businesses use inter-market tectonics to realise their ultimate *fingerspitzengefühl* capacity!"

It was the end of a long day, but it still wasn't over: we had an evening talk by Amelyosis's Chief Executive to sit through. A PowerPoint presentation on the screen behind him resumed the essential points of his incomprehensible argument: *corporate neurosurgery, neo-geo-economics, fish and chips, bongo marketing.*

"What the hell is *fingerspitzengefühl*?" I asked Nick, who was sitting beside me.

"It's German," he answered.

"I would never have guessed. What does it *mean?*"

"It describes... when you instinctively know

something. Literally, it's a tingling sensation you get in your fingers."

I was impressed. Nick really knew his professional jargon.

"So you understand what Cicero's talking about?" I asked.

"Of course. It's brilliant. It's totally visionary."

I felt like an idiot. Everyone was looking intelligently at Cicero, apparently following his every word. Was there an Amelyosis *phrase book* that I was supposed to have studied?

"So what exactly... *is* he saying?" I whispered to Nick.

"Nothing at all," he answered, "but he's doing it *brilliantly*. This is why the man is paid five million a year. He's taking management consultancy to another level. Listen and learn, James. Listen and learn."

I tried, but I found myself thinking about changing profession instead. Personally, I always liked the idea of being a carpenter. There's no money in it, of course, but it would be satisfying to make things – *real* things with a *real* function. Like bookshelves and tables. That would be cool.

At Amelyosis we sell the illusion of competence, pretending to understand other people's businesses. We are all charlatans – me, Nick, even Rueben Cicero – but our talent is to sound convincing. This is why it is important to be incomprehensible.

"–synergies of cappuccino capitalism!" Rueben Cicero continued effortlessly, "Because, believe me, ladies and gentlemen: today's high-definition TV is tomorrow's low-fat yoghurt! *Adapt, adaptify, adaptificate*!"

I looked away from Cicero as I put a hand over my mouth to camouflage a yawn. My eyes met those of the young female executive I saw on the beach yesterday. She was sitting a few seats away and smiling as she observed my boredom. She raised her eyebrow a fraction, questioningly, and I gestured toward Cicero, shaking my head to express my incomprehension. She laughed silently and then put two fingers in her mouth as if to vomit.

I think I am in love.

Day 3

I

TODAY, OPTIMUM TRAINING organised a rock-climbing competition. Again, not something I see us doing in a business environment, but on these training courses cynicism is illegal. We are here to bond. We are here to be team players. Unfortunately, Nick and me were on a team with an American guy named Spalding Barnes, who they say is some kind of financial genius: fantastic head for numbers, no head for heights.

Our opponents in the first round were a female team that included the girl from last night. I smiled across at her, hoping that I did not look too ridiculous in my orange harness and safety helmet. Somehow she managed to make the same equipment look sexy. Stylish, even. I don't know how it is some women can do that. Is it a question of attitude, or do you simply always look stylish if you have good legs? A mystery.

This was the first opportunity I had had to speak to her, but I suddenly had no idea what to say. Luckily for me, she took the initiative: leaving her two team-mates and walking toward me, coming up so close that she could speak without anyone else hearing.

"Your team-mate doesn't look too good," she said quietly, looking toward Spalding Barnes. Her voice had a slight accent – French, or maybe Italian, I thought. "Are you sure he can do this?"

I followed her eyes and noticed the pallor of Spalding's face as he stood at the bottom of the vertical rock-face, waiting for our turn to start. She was right. He was looking distinctly nauseous. I made a mental note to make sure that I was not underneath him on the climb.

"I'm not sure that *I* can do it, to be honest." I answered, "But it's not as if we have a choice, is it?"

She shrugged her shoulders.

"If he doesn't want to do it, he shouldn't do it," she answered simply, "It's not just dangerous for him, but for you too."

I felt a surge of pleasure at her concern for my well-being. She would probably have said the same thing to anyone else, but she said it to me and I chose to interpret that as a sign of intimacy.

"You're right." I said, "I'll go and see him. Do you think he can refuse to do it?"

"Of course he can," she answered, "It's not against the law, is it?"

Her English was generally excellent, but she had trouble pronouncing the word 'law' correctly, making it sound like 'low'. Definitely French, I decided.

II

"You've been analysing the competition, have you?" Nick asked as I rejoined him after speaking to the French girl, "That one looks in good physical shape. Did you discover if she's done any rock-climbing before?"

I looked at him, wondering if he was serious or not. We are all ambitious at Amelyosis, but I have never known anyone so intently focussed on his objectives as Nick Sark. Even the way he *walks* betrays his determination: almost military in its purpose, as if he is always going somewhere very specific, to do something very particular. Nick might stop on his way from A to B to share a joke with a colleague, but there is always something calculated about it – it is a conscious decision to engage in social bonding.

"I think she has, yes." I replied, deciding he was serious, "She says that we should be careful about Spalding Barnes. He looks like he might suffer from vertigo."

"Aha... I see. Clever. Good tactics," he mused to himself, "Don't you see, James? She's trying to psychologically destabilise you before the competition. Don't let that bitch get inside your head."

"No, I think she *really* is concerned about Spalding, Nick. And she's right – the man's skin is green."

Nick looked at Spalding, who was nervously

checking his equipment for the fifth or sixth time, and nodded slowly.

"He just needs some positive reassurance. Leave this to me," he said, stepping over toward him and putting his hand on Spalding's arm.

"Spalding, isn't it? The Houston office? Hi, I'm Nick. So, are you excited about the competition?"

"It... it... it's a challenge for me." Spalding answered.

"Absolutely. It's by challenging ourselves that we develop as individuals and grow!"

Spalding nodded robotically.

"Yes. Yes..." he said softly, looking up at the rock, "Or... die."

"*Whoa!*" Nick cried, "Negative attitude! Come on, Spalding, you're from Texas!"

A pained expression crossed Spalding's face.

"And that means I'm good at rock-climbing?"

"Texans are *courageous*, Spalding." Nick answered, "That's your brand image."

"Okay... Nick. Can I share a secret with you? " Spalding said, "As you know, Texas is big – about five times bigger than England. But you may not know that it is also, above all, very flat."

"No hills?"

"Flat, flat, flat," the American confirmed, "I have to tell you, Nick, if my Texan ancestors obtained a courageous... brand image, they did so on the *horizontal* plane."

Nick was not someone to be defeated so easily. There was a competition to win. Against girls.

"Okay, Spalding," he announced cheerfully, "the problem here is essentially psychological. The secret is *not* to think of it as a rock."

"Uh-huh. Okay. So what *is* it?" Spalding asked.

"That's not important. Use your imagination. Pretend it's a... gigantic female breast."

The three of us silently contemplated the large obstacle in front of us.

"I don't know, Nick," Spalding said finally, "I'm trying to use my imagination here, but frankly it just looks like a big... rock."

"He's right, Nick." I added, "It looks *nothing* like a breast. You have a very strange idea of female anatomy."

"Of course it doesn't look like a woman's breast, James, because it's a fucking big *rock!*" he snapped, losing control of his temper, "Are you suggesting that I have never seen a woman's *breast* before?"

"I don't know, Nick," I answered, "but you have to admit it was a bizarre choice of image."

"I thought John Wayne here might find the image of a breast to be comforting. Sorry. Clearly I was wrong." Nick turned to Spalding and snarled, "Let's try a different approach – if we lose this competition because of you, I am personally going to pull off your head and *shit down your neck, okay?*"

III

Having worked with Nick before, I am accustomed to his sudden explosions of rage. Spalding, to his credit, remained more good-humoured than most people probably would if a small Englishman threatened to defecate on them.

"Oka-a-ay," he answered, "I can see that you are... a highly-motivated individual."

I like that about Americans. Europeans say that they are impolite, but that is so untrue. In my experience, Americans are extremely polite. There is something elaborate and almost 19th century about the politeness of many Americans. They invent euphemisms for their euphemisms.

Think of all the creative terms that they have invented for the toilet.

They ask for the 'bathroom', for instance. Do they want a bath? Clearly not. Are you going to direct them to a room that *contains* a bath? Not usually. But there is a subtle association at work. They are letting you know that they wish to visit a room that has *plumbing*.

Alternatively, they will ask to use 'the rest-room'. Again, are they tired? Do they need to lay down upon your bed after a long journey across the Atlantic? Clearly not. They do not want rest, but *respite*. Again, a subtle connection.

I have trouble seeing the connection in the euphemism 'room of convenience'. If I *had* something called a 'room of convenience', I think it is where I would put my Hoover. But not me. People don't belong in a 'room of convenience'.

My conclusion is that American toilet euphemisms are systematically moving through every room in the house. When one room becomes too clearly associated with the toilet, despite not *having* a toilet, they move onto the next one. They cannot continue like this forever. Eventually, unless they lose all connection with reality and start asking how to get on the roof, there will be nowhere left for them to go *except* the toilet.

Perhaps this explains the most recent euphemism I heard: the 'comfort station'. Where did they get *that* from? The 'comfort station' is like some *imaginary* room or device they have invented. It sounds like it comes from a science-fiction film in which futuristic homes contain 'comfort stations' that will give you a body-massage while you do your business.

But I digress.

IV

"Don't look down!" Nick ordered.

"I'm *not* looking down!" Spalding shouted, "I'm just stuck, okay? I can't move."

"It's okay – we're a team." Nick answered, "I'm right behind you."

"For some reason, that does not reassure me."

The rock-climbing competition was not going well.

From my position at the front, I could see the posteriors of the rival team confidently ascending the rock. Spalding had lost motor control at a particularly inconvenient moment, when my arms and legs were spread against the rock like a bug on a car windscreen.

"Well, this is educational, isn't it?" I announced, the physical pain evident in my voice, "This is... this is *excellent* business training! Look at me, Nick – how do you like my impression of General Motors?"

"Do you think you're funny, James?" Nick shouted, "You're not funny."

"I tell you what *isn't* funny, Nick." I replied, "I'm not going to be able to hold on much longer..."

"Do you hear that, Spalding?" Nick said, "The man is going to let go if you don't move. We are all connected by a rope. There are *implications*."

It was no good. Spalding was completely petrified.

"I warn you: I am going to fall!" I shouted.

"Spalding! He's going to fall!" Nick shouted desperately, "Cut the rope! Cut the fucking rope!"

"I love you too, Nick." I grimaced.

He was right, however. But I realised that I didn't need to cut the rope because I could simply disconnect my harness. I held on as firmly as I could with my left hand, freeing my right hand to undo the D-clip. Once I was not tied to Spalding, I moved carefully across to a flat shelf on the rock-face where I could rest.

"So now what?" I shouted down.

That was when I realised that Spalding *had* fallen off.

V

By evening, I decided that I had bonded too much with my colleagues and went for a walk alone on the beach. There was a karaoke night organized and my absence would probably be noted, but if Amelyosis was supposed to be one big family then somebody should play the role of the moody adolescent, shouldn't they?

As the light from the hotel gradually diminished,

the only noises came from the jungle. There was no moon, and the sea was so calm that it was like a sheet of metal in the starlight. Somewhere, two or three hundred kilometres across the water, was India. The tiny island we were on, Iteepoa, was uninhabited except for the luxury hotel complex in which we were staying – there was no natural supply of fresh water, so humans had never colonised it.

For millennia, its coral reef prospered, its forest flourished, and the white sands of its beaches remained pure. Now it was home to one hundred and fifty Management Consultants singing bad versions of Beatles songs.

I sat down on the sand, suddenly hit by a depressing sense of the absurdity of the modern world. One day you are in London, the next on an island in the Indian Ocean – it has become like changing channels on a TV, so easy that nothing feels quite real anymore. I like to travel as much as most people, but I suspect that as we make the world smaller and less strange, we reduce our sense of self in proportion.

"Fucking ridiculous." I sighed, lying down on the sand.

Above me, there were more stars visible than I had ever imagined it was possible to see without a telescope. So many that there was almost no space left for darkness. I could even see the red and blue-coloured nebulae that I'd only ever seen in photographs before.

"You are talking about your rock-climbing, I presume." a familiar voice said from the darkness.

I sat up again in surprise and realised that the dark-haired girl, whose name I had discovered to be Marianne, was lying on the sand only a couple of metres away. In the darkness, I had almost walked on her.

"That *was* fairly ridiculous, I agree." I laughed, "But it wasn't what I had in mind."

"How is your team-mate, the American?"

"He's okay. He has a twisted ankle. Luckily he was only three metres from the ground when he fell. Nick will never forgive him, though."

"He should not have climbed," she said angrily, "Just because we work for Amelyosis, why does that give them the right to tell people to climb rocks?"

"That's what I keep asking myself: what am I

doing in the middle of the Indian Ocean, climbing rocks and eating bugs?"

"Do you wish you were at home?" she asked, rolling over to look at me, her head resting on her arm.

"Am I homesick? No. On the contrary. I think that's the problem – I wish I *was* homesick. I wish there was somewhere in the world that held that kind of significance for me. Do you know what I mean?"

"Not really," she said, "Home to me is a village in the centre of France where my parents live."

"Are you ever going back there?"

"Sure. Maybe one day." she answered, "I don't know. For the moment, I like not knowing."

"You're lucky." I told her, "I have zero connection to the town where I grew up. My parents retired to the countryside, and I lost contact with all my school-friends when I went away to university so the place has nothing for me now. That's what I mean: home is not a geographical place, but simply the physical space where my stuff is."

"Mmm... the cool nomad type, huh?" she asked mockingly.

"No, seriously – I'm not saying it's cool! I would *love* to have a connection to somewhere. I think human beings need that. In the past, we defined ourselves by geographical connection to the land: our valleys, our villages, our fields, our streets. We need *something* like that to give us a sense of who we are. That's why we have become so obsessed with material possessions, isn't it? We define ourselves by shopping. I am the contents of my fridge."

"Your *fridge?*" she laughed, "Why is the fridge so important?"

"A fridge says a lot about you, don't you think?"

"Not mine. There's nothing much in it!" she answered, "Does that signify that I am superficial?"

"No, it probably signifies that you don't cook."

"It's best for other people that I don't." she confessed with a smile, "In the past, I tried to cook meals for my boyfriend, but it always ended up in a big argument! In the end, I accepted that I am simply a disaster in the kitchen."

"So does he cook instead, your boyfriend?"

"Laurent? Are you *crazy?* No – he found himself another girl who doesn't burn the food or shout at him, and now they're getting married."

There was something about her smile as she looked at me that made my stomach tighten.

"Oh... sorry." I frowned, a little embarrassed, "Still, it sounds like you're probably better off without him."

"Probably." she sighed, running her fingers through her hair, "He was very good-looking, though."

"They're often the worst."

"Mmm, but it's so hard these days..."

"What – to find a reasonably attractive man who likes to cook?"

She cocked her head as she looked at me. I felt the knot harden in my stomach as I met her eyes.

"Do you know any?" she said.

Was she really flirting or just having fun? I never know the difference. Perhaps there *isn't* any difference. I don't know. But I did know that this was a chance that might never present itself again:

the two of us meeting in the darkness on a beach thousands of miles from home.

The surreal feeling of a moment ago had disappeared in her presence.

Suddenly, everything felt hyper-real. I told myself that I had to be brave, to take the plunge and risk everything on that one crucial question.

"Do you..." I asked, moving a little closer to her, "like beef teriyaki?"

She too drew closer, and stopped with a smile – waiting for a brief eternity to pass before she whispered, "As a matter of fact, I *love* beef teriyaki..."

Day 4

I

I WAS WOKEN by Marianne this morning.

"James – there's no power." she said, "None of the lights work. There's no water either."

I tried to lift my head from the pillow, but with little success.

"Oh my god..." I groaned, "does that mean there's no coffee? We have to listen to Cicero's presentation without *coffee*?"

I rolled over to see her looking every bit as gorgeous as I remembered, tying a bath-towel around herself.

"There's no shower, so I'm going for a swim in the sea." she said, "Coming?"

It was half-past six. Clearly, Marianne had only just met me, or else she'd have known that I would never consider going for a swim at half-past six in the morning. To my surprise, I found myself jumping out of bed, smiling "Sure" like this was the kind of thing I did every day.

The sun was just about to rise as we exited the silent hotel – a saffron glow was starting to turn the silver water gold on the horizon, but in the bay where the hotel was situated it still looked cold and unwelcoming.

"Come on." she called as I looked uncertainly at the water, "Or else we'll miss all the sharks!"

"Sharks? What do you mean *sharks*?"

"Sharks always hunt at dawn." she laughed, "Haven't you ever seen *Jaws?*"

She slipped off her bathrobe to reveal a black swimsuit with a white belt, and stepped forward from the beach, shouting "You're not scared, are you, James?" before diving into the water and swimming confidently away from the shore.

As a matter of fact, I was. Terrified. When I was a boy, my fear of sharks had been so total that it extended even to swimming pools. Even today, my fear of deep water is still so strong that some would call it a phobia.

Incorrectly, I think. Phobias are irrational. Large, man-eating fish are perfectly real.

The main hotel building was on the periphery of the forest, but a wooden pier reached out over the crystal waters of the bay on which there were a number of luxury chalets that were occupied by the senior management of Amelyosis. It was toward these that Marianne was swimming.

I could not let Marianne think me a coward, and so I followed her out into the bay, ignoring the fact that the theme music from *Jaws* had started playing in my head. She was a faster swimmer than me, but she stopped to wait once she reached the furthest of the chalets. I arrived a little out of breath, and took her in my arms to stop her from swimming off again.

The skin of her torso was cold against mine as we kicked our legs to stay afloat. The water was dark and deep. I imagined a deadly shape moving silently under our feet, attracted by the movement... and realised that I did not care. For the first time in my life, I was not scared of the sharks.

As I realised this, it made me think of something my mother used to say that I had never really understood: "You do not fall in love with someone because of the person they are. You fall in love with them because of the person they make *you*."

I was asking myself if Marianne could be that person when we heard the sound of footsteps above our heads. Someone was walking along the pier to the last of chalets, under which we were currently floating. The feet stopped and someone knocked at the door, calling,

"Mister Cicero? Are you awake, sir? I have some bad news."

II

The man's Indian accent denoted him as being one of the hotel staff, and he waited patiently before knocking on the door again – more insistently this time. We heard Cicero get out of bed and a muffled curse as he tried the lightswitch. His footsteps crossed the floor toward the door.

"Hey, I don't seem to have any light." he said in a tired voice, "Is the power out or something?"

"Temporarily, sir." the man replied, "This is why I am taking the liberty of waking you at this time – to apologise on behalf of the Iteepoa Luxury Eco-Resort and Conference Centre. We cannot be preparing the luxury breakfast buffet today because there is no power in the kitchens. Instead, we will be offering a range of cereals, muffins and fruit juices only, sir. This is the American Breakfast Menu. But without the coffee. Or the pancakes."

"Is your generator broken?"

"No, sir – I am happy to say that the problem does not come from the hotel generator, which is absolutely top-quality. But the generator is controlled by a computer server in Mumbai, and the problem is coming from there. This is a problem for the toilet system because the water uses electrical pumps–"

"Yeah, yeah, yeah. How long will it take to fix?"

"I'm sorry to say that I do not know, sir. I think it is a big problem because most of the radio stations are not working this morning. But you must please be telling your people about the problem with the hotel toilets because–"

"*Screw the toilets!* What do you mean there's no radio?"

"Most unfortunately, the only radio station we are receiving today is transmitting in Urdu, sir. The problem is, sir, my native language is Hindi, so I do not understand him very well. He keeps using the word *tabaahi,* which means 'break' or 'crash', I think."

"What sort of a crash?"

"I'm not sure – I have heard him say *hawaai jahaz,* which means plane. But I have also heard him use the word *'computer'.*"

"I assume that is Urdu for computer?"

"Yes, sir. So maybe he is talking about a plane crash or a computer crash, or maybe a plane is crashing *because* the computer is crashing. I don't know."

"So when will we know how long it is going to take for the power to come back?"

"We will know... *when* the power comes back, sir."

III

"Why are we here, people?" Rueben Cicero asked us all two hours later in the semi-dark conference centre, "To challenge ourselves! To develop as individuals! To strengthen our team spirit! This situation does not present us with a problem... It presents us with an *opportunity to excel!*"

Without the microphone to amplify his voice, and without the screen to transform his words into diagrams and bulletin points, Cicero was having to work harder than usual to convince everyone that he knew what he was talking about, and it showed when he took questions.

"What exactly has happened?" someone asked first.

"Personally, I don't think that is relevant. Too much information complicates the decision-making process." Cicero commented, "Fortunately, at the present time, we are not encumbered by data. I am excited by that. The facts are in flux."

There was a pause as everyone internally translated his reply: *I have no idea what has happened.*

"But the plane will be coming to take us back in two days' time, right?" someone asked.

"I don't think we should determine the parameters of our current reality in a chronocentric fashion." Cicero answered, "The present is the future."

"But my wife is about to have a baby," the man insisted.

"Congratulations." Cicero smiled, "This must be a particularly exciting situation for you. Are there any other interrogatives?"

"Yes." a woman said, "Is it true we cannot use the toilets?"

"Yes."

This raised a laugh because it was, without doubt, the most direct answer anyone had ever heard Cicero give.

"So what *do* we use?" she persisted.

"We use... our imagination."

Again, he got a laugh and the mood of tension in the hall was beginning to dissipate when Nick stood up to ask:

"Is Amelyosis prepared to guarantee our personal security?"

"I'm not sure that I understand your question, Mr...?"

"Sark. Nick Sark – London office." Nick said, "My question is simple, Mr. Cicero: what guarantee is there that we will all get off this island alive?"

There was a shocked silence, even Cicero being taken by surprise. Then he began to laugh:

"I didn't think the English were prone to melodrama, Mr. Sark."

Most of the audience began to laugh with him, but Nick raised his voice to shout over the noise:

"Have you checked our supply of drinking water, Mr. Cicero?"

"Um... not personally, no, but these are issues we will be looking into–"

"I have. Without electricity, the hotel's desalination plant is out of action. We have just under 500 litres of bottled mineral water – enough, according to my calculations, for a week at the most." he informed everyone, adding sarcastically, "Or is my approach too... *chronocentric*, Mr. Cicero?"

It was a bold move on Nick's part, a direct challenge to Cicero's authority. The hall was tense as we waited to see how he would react.

"As Chief Executive Officer of Amelyosis," Cicero began, "let me make one thing very, *very* clear–"

"There is no electricity, no phone signal, and no radio. Clearly, something *major* has happened in the world." Nick interrupted, "How do we know Amelyosis even *exists* anymore?"

"Amelyosis still exists, Mr. Sark, because we *are* Amelyosis!" Cicero shouted, finally losing his cool, "If you do not think *your* future lies with this company, then you are at liberty to resign. Now, since you have raised the issue, let's establish right now whether Amelyosis still exists, shall we? Can we have a show of hands, please – does anyone here *not* want to continue their collaboration with Amelyosis, or have any problem with the management structure in place?"

He waited, letting his gaze roam around the assembled executives for what seemed like an eternity, daring one of them to raise their hand. Not one did.

"Well, Mr. Sark..." he smiled, "Are you with the rest of us, or are we to consider you as self-employed from now on?"

IV

"Personally, I think it's a Babel Virus, don't you?" Nick declared to some of us as we left the conference room, "Nothing else could be this powerful."

While Marianne and I looked at one another in mutual incomprehension, the three other executives nodded their agreement with Nick. I waited for one of them to say something, but nobody did.

"Umm... this may be a stupid question, but what's a Babel Virus, Nick?" I asked.

"Ja-a-ames!" Nick sighed, rolling his eyes. The other executives laughed quietly.

"Oh... bullshit!" Marianne snapped, looking at them. I liked the way she pronounced 'bull' like *'boule'*. "So you all know what it is? Come on then – explain it to me!"

"Everyone knows what–" Nick began.

"*Pas toi, mon petit.*" Marianne interrupted, "I want to hear it from one of *these* guys."

The men looked from one to another, as if politely inviting each other to be the first to answer her.

"It's... um... really bad," one of them explained eventually. I recognised him as the one whose wife was about to have a baby.

"Vicious," the second added.

"Ugly," said the third.

Clearly, nobody had a clue what a Babel Virus was but, as professionals of bullshit, they were never going to admit that.

"Oh my god, is it contagious?" Marianne asked in mock-terror.

"For god's sake!" Nick interrupted, "You're all as hopeless as each other! The Babel is the Holy Grail of hackers. It is a binary epidemic that secretly penetrates the entire world's communications networks, and then, when the order is given, crashes everything simultaneously: satellites, defence systems, banks, power plants, transport, the web... *everything!*"

"Why would someone do that?" I asked, "Are they stupid? That's a... really *bad* idea. Who would want to do that?"

"The Chinese, of course." Nick said, as sure of his opinion as always, "They've been preparing for a computer war for years now. All computer systems infected with a Babel Virus would effectively be united into one single network, under their control. In one move, they take over the world: checkmate."

"So that's it, then?" I said, "While we were singing karaoke versions of The Beatles, the Chinese took over the world?"

Something about this 'Babel Virus' seemed familiar to me. I'd heard about it on TV, I thought. But not the news. Where was it? Suddenly I remembered – it was in an episode of an American TV series, a comedy about a man who works in a computer shop.

"Nick..." I ventured once we were alone. I asked him if he watched the TV show in question.

We were walking toward the beach. His foot hesitated almost imperceptibly in mid-air.

"No." he answered. "Never."

Day 6

I

DUE TO THE CRISIS, Cicero and the senior management have decided to reorganise us into different groups. The biggest group, of which Nick and I are both part, is the Carbon-Sourcing Directorate. This means that our job is to collect firewood.

There is plenty of wood in the forest. That is not the problem. The problem is that the only sharp instruments we have are kitchen utensils.

"Meanwhile, Cicero and the senior managers remain on the beach to 'develop strategy'," one of my carbon-sourcing colleagues complained to me as we worked in the jungle heat. "The hardest work they have is opening an Evian bottle."

"Some of those bottle-tops can be pretty difficult. You know, the ones that just keep going round and round?" I said. "Anyway, what do you expect from senior management?"

"They better develop a damned good strategy, that's all I can say," he grumbled.

There are two rival theories about our situation. One theory is that this is all a test and Amelyosis itself arranged for the power and communications to be lost. That is why they decided to hold the training course on this island: it is an easy environment for them to create the illusion of a catastrophe.

The people who favour this explanation disagree about how we should react: do we continue as if the situation is real, or do we change the script and challenge Cicero's authority?

"It's a classic business problem," one of my colleagues pointed out, "in an unfavourable economic situation, should one adopt a defensive or offensive business strategy?"

"Or no strategy at all." I answered.

He narrowed his eyes at me, uncertain of what I was saying.

"What are you suggesting?"

"Nothing at all. Maybe we should just sunbathe and hope that someone comes to rescue us."

"Do you know something that you're not telling me?"

"No, I'm just saying that I'd rather be sunbathing than collecting firewood."

"You're thinking of a Taoist approach, aren't you?" he answered finally, "Lao Tzu says the wind will break the tree, but the reed will bend no matter how hard the wind blows? True strength is in offering no resistance?"

"Lao Tzu." I nodded, "The man."

"You're good. I like your way of thinking."

I would probably believe this was all a test if Marianne and I had not been swimming underneath Cicero's chalet when the hotel manager told him about the problem. Cicero's surprise was sincere and, anyway, he didn't *know* anyone was there to hear him. So if it really was a test, that would imply that Optimum Training didn't tell him what was on the programme.

This is possible.

Then there is another theory that is proving popular...

"Have you heard the rumour? Everyone says that the Chinese have taken over the world." another co-worker confided to me as we carried wood back to the beach. "The bastards have got a Baby Virus."

"A Baby Virus?" I asked, "How do you know?"

"Well, it's obvious, isn't it? Look at how many Chinese there are! A billion! Clearly, the bastards have had a Baby Virus for years now."

II

As the day grew older, I began to notice people reacting to Nick as if he was our unofficial leader. I think that, in their resentment of the senior management, people naturally turned to Nick because he was the only person who had been courageous enough to challenge Cicero.

By the end of the day, we had collected a large supply of firewood and, perhaps sensing tension in the air, Cicero announced that we would celebrate with a big beach party. The hotel staff had removed all the most perishable items from the kitchen freezers and prepared them for barbequeing over open fires. Large quantities of wine, beer and spirits were produced, and a battery-powered CD player provided music as darkness fell.

It almost worked. We formed small groups and gathered around separate fires to cook our meat on long sticks. With the sound of the sea, the music and the alcohol, we began to forget the gravity of our situation. Wasn't this exactly the life most people dreamed of – a barbeque on a tropical beach in the Indian Ocean? Gradually, the conversation became more animated and people regained their sense of humour.

As the light of the fires softened the hard, ambitious faces of my colleagues, I felt as if we *were* all part of one team, that Amelyosis *did* represent a bond between us all. With Marianne sitting beside me, and my hand stroking her back in the secrecy of the dark, I felt a sudden surge of affection for everyone there, and was proud to be a part of this team. I was happy. But then, like everyone else, I'd had a lot to drink.

Which is probably why none of us responded very quickly when somebody shouted "*Fire! The hotel's on fire!*".

Day 7

I

NOBODY KNOWS *who* started the fire, but it's obvious how it started: without any electric light to see their way inside the hotel, people started using burning torches from the barbeque fires. As the party progressed and everyone got drunker, someone accidentally barbequed the hotel. I don't judge. Personally, I overcooked my sausage.

The Iteepoa Hotel and Conference Centre was one of those wonderful, designer eco-resorts where everything was built out of natural, environmentally-friendly materials. Wood, principally.

Of course, the hotel conformed to the strictest contemporary standards of safety: there were ceiling sprinklers in case of a fire. Unfortunately, without electricity, there were no pumps, and no water.

Well, no water. There *was* the Indian Ocean just a few metres away, but that was in the wrong position. It was a major logistical problem. Sorry – opportunity. Cicero organised a human chain to transport as much of the Indian Ocean as possible into the hotel, but since we were only using flower pots, kitchen casseroles and vases, the flow of water was insufficient. As it became obvious that the combat was lost, people began running crazily into the burning building to save their possessions.

"We need to get the food and water from the *kitchens,* you idiots!" Nick shouted.

We organised a new human chain whose objective was to transport as much Evian and breakfast muesli as possible. We saved most of it before the kitchen caught fire and were about to return one last time when the hotel manager came running around the side of the building, shouting,

"Stay back! The fire is reaching the fuel reserve for the generator! The whole hotel is going to–"

But then it did.

II

As dawn rose this morning over the smoking ruins of the Iteepoa Luxury Hotel and Conference Centre, the sum total of my possessions were as follows: 1 pair of Converse shoes (dirty), 1 pair of underpants (dirty), 1 pair of socks (smelly), 1 pair of Chinos (torn), 1 white t-shirt (torn), 1 mobile phone (no signal), and 1 large butcher's knife. The cool nomad type it is, then.

Others managed to save more for themselves before the fire engulfed the hotel, but when I looked at the items laid out on the sand – Macbooks and laptop PCs, designer suits and dresses, toiletries, make-up bags, Vuitton bags, phones and mp3 players – I felt little regret for what I had lost. The beach looked like the ruin of some distant civilization: a jigsaw of objects with no cultural context to explain them.

According to this morning's head count, it seems that the explosion killed six Amelyosis employees and several of the hotel staff, but nobody knows exactly how many because the only person who might have been able to say, the hotel manager, is toast. Perhaps most tragically of all, from our point of view, the survival guide from Optimum Training is not among the survivors. This is unfortunate because he had yet to teach us what culinary delights the island contains *apart* from Samson Bugs.

"This is the day that the plane is supposed to come back for us." Marianne reminded me as we walked away from the devastation on the beach.

"Do you think it's going to come?" I asked. "Do you think it's possible that the whole crisis was just part of the training programme?"

She looked out across the ocean. It was another beautiful day, the sky a rich blue without a cloud in sight.

"Look at the sky." she answered, "Perfect blue. Not a single vapour trail has crossed it for three days. Right now, the only way off this island is on a boat."

III

The only buildings left intact by the fire are the chalets built over the water, to which Cicero and the rest of the senior management retreated to 'discuss strategy'. They were in there all morning – a sign, in my opinion, that they had no idea what to do.

I have a theory about business meetings: the longer they go on, the less will be decided. In my experience as a consultant, I've seen it a hundred times. The companies that have the longest, most numerous meetings are the ones that are in trouble. Their business is going badly and the management don't know what to do, so instead of taking action they multiply the number of meetings and committees. It's an illusion to make everyone feel that the situation is under control: *something* must come of all this talking. Generally, the opposite is true. In a well-organised company with good managers, everyone is too busy to waste time on meetings.

Everyone else remained on the beach, too shocked by the enormity of what had happened to do anything but sit on the sand and hope for a miracle: the vapour trail of a jet in the sky. Marianne and I, however, decided to build ourselves a structure for the coming night. With the hotel gone, and not enough room in the chalets for everyone, most people are going to be sleeping on the sand. We chose a location a few hundred metres from the ruins of the hotel, and began to collect sticks and palm leaves for a little refuge.

I know it sounds impossible, given the gravity of our situation, but I was strangely happy. Compared to everything else in my life, this made sense: to be creating a home, even if it was only out of palm leaves. And even though we are totally isolated, without enough food or water to survive for more than a few days, I was not alone. I was doing this with somebody.

At long last, I was part of a team.

IV

The strategy meeting went on all day. Based upon my experience of companies in difficulty, this clearly indicates that we are fucked.

When, at last, people began to emerge from Cicero's chalet, their faces did not inspire confidence – they instantly broke up into small groups and continued talking, their eyes turning anxiously toward other groups. The great Amelyosis tribe was starting to disintegrate, I realised.

And then, to my surprise, someone walked out of the chalet in the company of Cicero himself. Someone who should not even have *been* at the meeting: Nick. They both nodded in agreement, and shook hands. In fact, they did more than shake hands: they also touched each other on the arm. The body language could not have been clearer.

Nick turned to walk away, and I noticed something different about him as he moved slowly along the jetty toward the beach. At first I couldn't define it, but then I realised that it was his walk that had changed – he no longer had that email urgency about him, but proceeded along the pier at a new, slower pace. He measured each step as if savouring the sound of his feet upon the wooden deck, brushing the cinders from last night's fire from his jacket as he went. He reached the end of the pier and stepped onto the sand, the familiar smile spreading like soft butter across his face as he saw me watching him.

"James." he said, "What a beautiful day it is, isn't it?"

"I suppose one should look on the bright side." I answered, "You've been with Cicero?"

"Yes." he nodded, speaking with a calm gravity, "Cicero has realised that Amelyosis's management structure needs to adapt to the current environment. He has asked me to assume the post of Vice-President of Resource Management. I have accepted."

"Resource Management?" I frowned, "What resources? Muesli resources?"

He placed a hand on my shoulder and looked me in the eye, unable to resist smiling:

"Muesli Resources. Water Resources. Human Resources." he said, "From now on, James, things on this island will be done *our* way!"

At first, I was flattered by the way he included me in the picture. I thought he was treating me as his equal. But then he patted me on the back and said,

"I'm going to need you beside me, James. I need people I can rely on."

"Oh... so do I get a promotion, too?" I joked.

"That's entirely possible." he answered, taking me seriously, "There's going to be a lot of changes at Amelyosis, James. A lot of opportunities for someone with the right attitude."

"Opportunities?" I frowned, "Nick – we're marooned in the Indian Ocean. There's no power, no water, and we just burned down the only hotel on the island! I don't think this is exactly a *professional* situation!"

He raised an eyebrow, clearly surprised by my attitude.

"On the contrary, James." he answered coolly, "Our professionalism is the only thing that will save us."

Day 10

I

REUBEN CICERO may still be nominally in charge of Amelyosis, but it has become clear to everyone that Nick, in his new role as Vice-President of Resource Management, holds the real power. Indeed, little has been seen of Cicero and the other board members since the fire. They retired to their chalets, preferring to delegate responsibility.

Nick made an impressive start. The first thing people want in a crisis is a strong leader to make them feel secure. In this, Nick excelled – he was energetic, enthusiastic and, above all, he was completely sure of himself. Apart from me, not many people on the island have ever worked with Nick before, and so they do not know that he has no *other* mode of existence.

Nick is equally sure of everything: the planet is spherical, Germans make the best cars, London is the greatest city in the world, President Kennedy was assassinated by the CIA, Coke is better than Pepsi, there are no UFOs, and one should put the milk into one's cup *before* pouring the tea. Anybody who thinks otherwise is wrong. Just *wrong*. Nick despairs of people who do not understand this.

Of all the different strengths a person can have, I think certainty in oneself is the most powerful. The problem, of course, is that only megalomaniacs and idiots are that sure of themselves.

II

We saved a good amount of food, principally comprised of bags of muesli. Nick arranged for that and all the water to be moved to one of the chalets, and placed an executive on permanent watch over it. This, he said, was to keep it safe. It also consolidated his control.

As it happened, we managed to resolve the water problem quite rapidly. Using materials recuperated from the ruins of the kitchen, we built a distillation plant that boiled sea-water over a fire, and deposited drinking water in a bathtub. The design was mine, as a matter of fact, but Nick somehow ended up believing it was his idea. It has always been a talent of his.

Food was a more difficult question. Nick's first strategy was to declare that we would live off fish from the coral reef. This seemed unrealistic to me.

To be honest, I've never understood the attraction of fishing. Yes, I realise that it is a tranquil, meditative activity, but it seems to me that fishermen almost never actually catch fish. These are people who have devoted *thousands* of hours to their pescatorial quest. They have so completely denied themselves the pleasures of home, family and human company that, if fishing were a spiritual belief, they would be the equivalent of ascetic hermits. I can only assume, therefore, that the attraction of fishing is precisely that fish are either too clever or too stupid to eat the bait that fishermen offer them, so justifying the long hours these men absent themselves from their families.

"Don't you think it's a little ambitious for us to catch fish, Nick?" I suggested, "The island must have something better than Samson Bugs on it."

"Ambition is the key to success!" he declared.

"Ye-e-s..." I agreed, not wanting to seem too negative, "But ambition is also an essential ingredient of *failure,* when you think about it."

I saw his eyes darken as the anger rose. Nick was not somebody who thought criticism to be constructive.

"The decision has been taken," he said, "We are not going to change direction now. It is everyone's duty to implement the strategy and make it a success."

II

Dozens of us at a time would go snorkelling in the coral reef, hunting with home-made spears – which was fun, at first, although I think the fish had more fun than we did. One team after another returned with nothing to show for their efforts. Despite this, Nick did not decide his strategy was wrong – the problem was our fishing. We needed to work harder, he said.

"I'm scared of your friend Nick." Marianne announced this evening, when we were alone on the beach, "He's dangerous."

"Dangerous? What makes you say that?"

"I don't know. I can sense it, that's all. It was a mistake for Cicero to put him in charge."

Even though she knew that we were far from the rest of the group and there was nobody who could hear our conversation, Marianne looked around carefully to check that we were truly alone before speaking. The light of the fire coloured her perfect skin bronze, her eyes reflected its dancing flames as she stared at me.

"We need to get off the island." she said.

"We're two hundred miles from the mainland!" I laughed, "It'd be crazy to try *sailing* to India!"

"Refugees do it."

"We don't even have a boat!"

She took hold of my hands, tracing her fingers over the damaged skin of my palms – the skin of an executive who, until recently, had never done a real day's work in his life.

"You said that you would have liked to be a carpenter, didn't you?"

I sensed myself weakening. That is what love does to you.

"Even if the currents took us in the right direction, which is by no means certain, we'd probably die of thirst and starvation in the middle of the ocean!" I protested, "And what if we were caught in a storm?"

"I know what you say is true, but I don't think we can stay here." She insisted, kissing my hand, "Trust me. I can feel that something terrible is going to happen."

Day 12

I

IT IS NOW FIVE DAYS since the plane was supposed to collect us, and still there is no sign of rescue. A strange atmosphere has come over the company: under Nick's command, Amelyosis has become an almost militaristic organization. People do not question orders. They ignore their doubts, do as they are told, and hope that they will live.

I am possibly the only person who is still able to talk to Nick as an equal. Perhaps because he has known me for longer than anyone else, I am able to say things to him that would provoke paroxysms of fury if it came from anyone else.

"I've decided on a new approach to get everybody working to the best of their abilities." he announced enthusiastically when I saw him this morning.

"But they already are doing that." I pointed out. "Everybody is collecting firewood, hunting for food, building new shelters – nobody is lying on the beach, Nick!"

"It's not enough. We need more food." he frowned, "I've decided to introduce a new system of rewards for Performance Excellation. From now on, those who work the hardest will receive a larger ration of muesli than the others."

I thought about this for a moment, and then pointed out,

"You can't do that, Nick. We can't raise the rations above the current level because our supplies will run out too fast. Until we develop new sources of food, we need to make the muesli last as long as possible."

He sucked in his cheeks, which was something he did when irritated, and then announced,

"Very well. Have it your way. We shall *halve* the rations of those who don't work productively enough."

"You can't do that!"

"What's the matter now?" he shouted, "*You're* the one who said I couldn't give our best people more food!"

"If we make the rations any smaller, Nick, people won't have enough to eat!"

"These are hard times." he said, "We have to be realistic about the situation. In the world of business, we all accept that a company cannot afford to retain ineffective employees, don't we? This is no different – here on this island, their salary is paid in food and water, and they must expect to lose that salary if their performance drops below the required level. We are not a charity, James!"

"The food is *not* their salary, Nick! The food is to keep us all alive – you have no right to give less to some than to others!"

"Excuse me, but who *paid* for that food, James? Amelyosis! It is company food, and will be distributed as a reward to those who work hard *for* the company! This is no different to the rules of business."

"If the company doesn't exist anymore, then the food belongs to nobody!"

“Who said Amelyosis doesn’t exist!” he exploded aggressively, coming forward until his face was only inches from mine.

“Well... you did,” I reminded him. “You said it to Cicero when we first lost the power.”

For an instant, Nick was struck dumb. His mouth went to speak, but no words came out. He was staring at me with such outright fury that I found it hard to keep my eyes locked on his, but I forced myself to do so, knowing that to look down now would be a form of submission despite the fact that I was clearly right.

“This isn’t a case of people losing their jobs, Nick.” I continued in as calm a voice as I could manage, “They could lose their *lives!*”

“I agree. The business climate *has* evolved dramatically,” he said quietly, “but the reality of life remains the same. If we were back home, and people lost their jobs, then wouldn’t the same question of how to feed themselves arise? Here, the connection is simply more... immediate. We are faced with difficult economic conditions that oblige us to adopt a new strategy. Greater effort is required from us all. It is up to each person to decide whether they are with us, or whether they wish to walk out the door."

"Walk out the *door*, Nick?" I laughed, savouring the irony of the phrase he had chosen, "In case you've forgotten, we are living on the beach – or perhaps you think that we have simply relocated to a new, open-plan office space?"

"Your attitude is not constructive, James." he reprimanded me, "I expect better from you."

II

I thought that Nick's new strategy for Performance Excellation would cause a rebellion among the Amelyosis executives, but I was wrong. Some, like me, thought it was obviously unjust that the strongest should receive twice as much food as others, but there were plenty of people who supported his policy, arguing that the *real* injustice would be for the less productive members to receive the same reward as everyone else.

Above all, however, I think that Nick generated support for his plan by offering people a sacrifice: as part of the Performance Excellation programme, Nick terminated the privileges enjoyed by Cicero and the senior management. From now on, they will work like everyone else.

Marianne, to my surprise, is not against Nick on this matter:

"In the end it will be the same!" she argued as we sat by our fire, some way down the beach from the main group, "Ultimately, the strongest will survive – that is Nature. Only a fool pretends otherwise. We do not have enough food and may not be rescued before it runs out. Nick cannot change reality!"

"That's *exactly* what humans do – we change reality!" I said, "That is why we consider ourselves better than other animals. We don't accept Nature's laws."

"That's just an illusion! Sure, we *try* to change reality, but at what cost? Look at what we've done to the planet! Look at the killing! In the end, we have not *changed* the reality of Nature at all – we have simply proved ourselves stronger than every *other* creature. All of our victories have come at a cost to something or someone else!"

Part of me accepted that Marianne was right: if

the situation continued to deteriorate, we needed to prepare a means of escape. I could see several problems, however. For one thing, I could not build a boat, so our vessel would have to be a simple raft big enough to support the two of us. But I could not build a raft without attracting attention and an 'excellent performer' should not be planning escape. If we were not careful, we would be on half-rations.

Luckily, we Amelyosis executives are supposed to think outside the box.

"I've decided that we're going to build ourselves a hut," I announced.

"But we have a shelter already, James," she frowned. "Why waste–"

"You don't understand," I interrupted her. "This is not an ordinary hut."

Lowering my voice to be sure we could not be overheard, I began to draw a picture of my idea in the sand. The hut would be built in bamboo tied together with vines – there would be a roof, held up with a strong central column. When turned upside down, however, the hut became a raft. The walls would be made from woven palm leaves attached to a light-weight bamboo structure that could, ultimately, become a sail.

This is what Rueben Cicero meant by Proactive Multifunctionality, I think. We are adapting ourselves for the challenges of the modern world.

Day 17

I

SPALDING BARNES WAS FIRED from Amelyosis today. Although he has been working hard, his twisted ankle has been a handicap. He has been failing to meet his Productivity Targets, and so his muesli ration had already been halved. Unsurprisingly, the less he eats, the weaker he becomes, and his work has suffered in consequence. Today, Cicero announced that his contract has been terminated, but I'm sure that the decision was entirely Nick's: he has probably never forgiven Spalding for the rock-climbing catastrophe.

We all knew that something bad was going to happen to him when he was called to Cicero's chalet, but I don't think any of us thought they would be so cruel as to make him redundant. And we were right. It was presented as a voluntary departure, of course.

"You want me to *resign?*" Spalding laughed, "Get real! I'll die! How am I going to eat?"

"We're offering you a generous severance package," Cicero explained, "the terms of which are as follows – your services will no longer be required, but you will be paid a quarter muesli salary for the next month or for the entire duration of our stay on this island, depending on which period of time is the shorter. In return, you will respect the 'no competition' clause of your contract until we leave the island."

"No competition?" he laughed, "What – I'm not supposed to start a Management *Consultancy* on the island?"

"That is correct." Cicero confirmed, "Or go fishing."

"*Fishing?*"

"Amelyosis is expanding and evolving, Spalding." Nick explained, "We are now Amelyosis, specialists in Corporate Solutions and *Fishing*.

Obviously, any fishing activity on your part will negate the terms of the severance package and your muesli salary will be suspended immediately."

"So I'm supposed to survive off Samson Bugs, am I?" he said angrily, "Is that it, or is there more?"

"That's it." Nick answered, "Except, of course, we have to ask you to vacate the company premises immediately."

"Premises? What fucking premises?" Spalding shouted, "We're on a beach on a tropical island! Where are the damned *premises?*"

That was when we discovered that Nick had been busier than we realised. He had ordered a team of executives to delineate the exact area of Amelyosis's premises by placing a line of rocks across the sand from the forest to the water five hundred metres either side of the ruins of the hotel. Anybody who had been made redundant, it was announced, was not allowed to cross this line.

Spalding accepted the voluntary redundancy because he understood the alternative was probably worse – Nick would work him to death. He was given a small sack of muesli that represented an entire week's salary, and escorted off company premises.

The line that Spalding is not allowed to cross is not far from the spot where Marianne and I are building our raft. He sat on the beach all day, just watching us work. He didn't hunt for bugs or build himself a shelter for the night. He just sat there, watching, like a man who has decided that he is going to die.

I would like to be able to say that we will help him, but we will not. We are guarding as much of our rations as we can in reserve for when we launch the raft.

II

The shock of Amelyosis's first redundancy on the island was immediately followed by another shock as Nick addressed the rest of us in a General Assembly.

"I have a couple of announcements." he began, looking down at his notes. "As some of you may know, Spalding Barnes has chosen to pursue other career options. Although we regret every departure from Amelyosis Corporate Solutions & Fishing, we have to accept that the economic climate is getting harsher: muesli supplies are going down, while our fish-based activities are still under-performing. Today, there is no room for those who are not prepared to work."

The Conference Room having suffered marginally less damage than the rest of the hotel, there was still a presentation chart on which he was able to write with a marker pen. He went over to it, pen in hand.

"If Amelyosis is to survive – and it *has* to survive – then we must concentrate on the core of our business." he said, drawing a big picture of a fish and underlining it for emphasis. "The future is *fish,* ladies and gentlemen!"

He rapidly drew lots of other, smaller fish all over the paper, declaring, "*Fish! Fish! Fish!*"

Marianne and I looked at each other, wide-eyed. Fish, fish, fish. At least it made a refreshing change from Cicero's impenetrable rhetoric.

"Now, as we... recenter on this core business area, not *everyone* is going to find their place in the new Amelyosis." he continued, "Those without good fishing skills may do better to consider accepting the same, generous severance package that Spalding Barnes was offered. It's a good deal, and available to anyone who has not been achieving his performance targets."

There was a murmur of outrage from around the assembled executives. The fact was that very few people were good enough at fishing to consider themselves safe.

"*Second* announcement!" Nick shouted, raising his hands for silence, "Obviously, in the current climate, it is essential that we maintain *unity* and a positive focus on the future. A small number of negative individuals can demotivate the entire team. This we cannot tolerate. Therefore, I have appointed a team of Strategy Compliance Executives to help keep order. Gentlemen, if you would please stand up..."

Fifteen of the largest, most physically impressive specimens of manhood on the island stood up at this point so that everyone could see who it was Nick was talking about.

"The Strategy Compliance Executives are here for *your* safety. They have my full authority to intervene in any dispute between Amelyosis employees and debrief those responsible. Any use of physical force will be met with an appropriate response by them, and to this end they will be entitled to carry defensive weapons. Are there any questions?"

A stunned silence greeted his announcement. I thought that I was still closer to Nick than anyone else was, but he hadn't told even me about this. Marianne and I looked at one another at the back of the briefing area.

"What did I tell you?" she said.

"Okay," I answered. "We need to finish our raft."

Day 19

I

IT IS HARD TO BELIEVE that it is less than three weeks since we came on this training course. Life before the island seems like a dream now, and just as a dream stops making sense when you wake up from it, life as we lived it three weeks ago seems impossibly absurd to me now.

Low-calorie desserts? Stiletto heels? SUVs? Football matches? Swarovski crystals? Phone apps? Ritalin? Nespresso capsules, for fuck's sake! How absurd is a world with Nespresso capsules? In a special presentation box. And yet we thought it was great. Desirable. Like George Clooney.

Do you want to know what *is* normal? Do you want to know what is *real?* It's this:

I am the only one in the meeting who is not a Strategy Compliance Executive. Cicero and the others are gone now – they've accepted severance packages. Nick no longer needs them now that he has his own police force.

To be honest, I don't know why he still trusts me, but he does. I suppose I am the connection between what is happening here on the island and life as we knew it before. If I am here, beside him, then there is a way back to the place where George Clooney sells us our Nespresso capsules.

Nick has been explaining that, even with all the redundancies, Amelyosis Corporate Solutions & Fishing is still not operating efficiently enough. He shows us a graph with two lines – one shows our muesli supplies descending, the other shows our fish supplies rising.

"At our present rate of progress," he says, "we will all die of starvation before we achieve self-sufficiency. Time is *not* on our side."

He turns over the page on his flip-chart to show us a new graph on which the muesli line was no longer descending as fast, but the fish line was not ascending so fast either.

"By managing our resources more effectively, we *can* marginally improve our chances of survival." he announces rapidly, "This, for instance, is the graph if we downsize by a further 30%."

"It's still not enough." I comment, noting that the lines crossed three or four weeks into the future.

"Precisely, James!" he smiles, "It's not enough. We have reached the point where any further redundancies will reduce our efficiency because there will be less people catching fish. Therefore, we need a different strategy. We need blue sky thinking!"

He turns the page to show us a new graph, the same as the one before, but with a third line joining the other two – a line that begins high and stays high.

"What's that line?" I ask, "Please don't tell me it's Samson Bugs."

"No, it is the meat supply." Nick answers.

"Meat? *What* meat supply? " I frown, looking around the room. "There's no meat supply."

A few of the Strategy Compliance Executives look down at the floor rather than meet my eye.

"James." Nick answers, rolling his eyes, "Jamie, Jamie, Jamie... you need to think outside the box. The situation is desperate. I want you to think carefully about the expression 'Human Resources'..."

II

Marianne and I turn our raft the right side up late at night, dragging it across the sand to the water. We are as quiet as possible, so as not to alert anyone, but we do not escape the attention of Spalding Barnes, sitting in his usual spot on the beach. I look at him, wondering if he is going to raise the alarm, but he just shakes his head at me and raises his hand to wave goodbye. I walk over to shake his hand.

"Good-bye, Spalding." I say, "I'm sorry that we can't take you with us."

"It's okay." he answers, "I hope you make it."

"Thanks."

I go to walk back down to the water, but realise that I cannot leave without saying anything. Slowly, I turn back round and take the butcher's knife from my belt, offering it to him.

"Take this." I say, "And, Spalding, listen: you

might want to send an urgent memo round the company. Nick is planning to start eating people when the muesli runs out. That will be very soon."

I leave him, and walk into the water. Pushing the raft in front of us, we swim across the bay toward the end of the jetty, tying off just below the chalet in which the muesli is being kept. Nobody has anticipated that a thief could come from the sea, and so I am able to climb up and in through a window. Silently, I drop the bags of muesli and bottles of water down to Marianne. All of them. And then I set fire to chalet before dropping back down to the raft: the jetty is a good defensive position, and a symbol of Nick's power that needs to be destroyed just like the hotel.

We are already a hundred metres or more away before the fire is noticed. We see Nick and the Strategy Compliance Executives running in and out, and can hear their voices as clearly across the water as if we are standing just beside them, but we are already invisible in the darkness of the sea. On the beach, I can see other points of fire starting to come together as Spalding spreads the news about the new interpretation of Human Resources.

So you see, we are not the good guys, Marianne and me. We are not necessarily even the winners – two hundred miles of water lie between us and the land, and it may be that we will die out here in the open sea. But we have a chance. We have a strategy.

And I do not feel bad about stealing all the food, because I did it for Marianne. I will do anything to save her, sacrifice anyone. That is the nature of love, and I do not regret anything that I do in her name. If necessary, I will sacrifice myself. Throw myself to the sharks.

People say nature is cruel, and humans are violent.

People say business is savage, and nice guys do not win.

People say only the strong survive.

Maybe all these things are true. I don't know. All I know is that in every human heart there is something stronger and, if necessary, more savage than any wild beast.

Lovers are the true barbarians. That is why love conquers.

If you enjoyed this book, don't miss the other titles from the **paper planes** collection.

Here is an excerpt from:

The Ghost Marriage

Peter May

Chapter 1

I

SWEET THOUGH IT WAS, the perfume of the incense could not disguise the odour of putrefying flesh. And the summer heat was not helping.

Two human cadavers were at the back of the room on a long table, surrounded by bowls of fresh fruit, boiled eggs in bowls of rice, *dim sum* still warm from the steamer, and a bottle of chilled white wine running with condensation.

The guests assembled at the far side of the room, near the window with a view on to the *siheyuan* courtyard. Children were playing in the *hutong* beyond, ignorant of the bizarre marriage ceremony taking place behind the high walls.

Paper effigies of the dead man and woman stood before the altar. A gong sounded in the hands of the priest, and with a movement of his red robe he placed a ring on the finger of the paper man. From the back of the observers, Feng Qi watched as the dead boy's mother now placed a ring on the paper finger of her son's wife. Feng Qi's eyes returned nervously to the cadaver of the dead girl, whose face was troublingly familiar.

II

The No. 1 Kindergarten in Anzhenxili, was not far from the No. 3 Ring Road, just north of Tiananmen, and the Forbidden City. As she waited for Li Jon, Margaret gazed from a window across the almost unrecognisable cityscape of post-olympic Beijing, reflecting on how rapidly much of this city had transformed itself from mediaeval to ultra-modern in the ten years since she first arrived.

She turned at the sound of children's voices filled with the euphoria of freedom after a long day of educational incarceration. Li Jon wrapped himself around her legs, and she lifted him up into her arms: something she would not be able to do for very much longer. He was growing like bamboo. She brushed dark hair from his eyes, and saw only his father in him: fine Chinese features that owed nothing to her fair-haired, blue-eyed Celtic heritage. But he had, she knew, inherited his mother's fiery, querulous spirit, and she took pleasure from his father's frustration that he had not transmitted to his son more of his gentle, Chinese fatalism.

"Did you get my iPod, mommy?" He spoke English with her distinctive American accent. But, also, Chinese like a native. Both she and Li spoke to their son in their native tongues, sending him to this bilingual kindergarten where he would learn to be a citizen of the world – bridging the cultural divide that had so often caused misunderstanding and conflict between his parents.

"Sure I did, honey. It's waiting for you back at the apartment."

He descended from her arms and took her hand, impatient to be home as soon as possible.

But he was forced to temper his excitement by

a lady who intercepted them at the front door. She wore blue overalls, and a white cloth cap, a few strands of greasy black hair hanging down from one side of it. Her hands were red and callused; her flat, peasant face rough and weathered, with troubled dark eyes. Margaret had seen her before, washing the floor of the lobby with slow, languid movements of her mop.

"Sorry to trouble you, lady." She was strangely formal, half bowing, almost deferential. "They tell me you are wife of Section Chief Li Yan."

Margaret took satisfaction from exercising her increasing skill in Chinese "Then I am sorry to say they tell you wrong." The woman's disappointment was almost palpable, and Margaret immediately regretted her abruptness. She added quickly, "An American woman is not permitted to marry a serving Chinese police officer." She pulled the child at her side a little closer. "But Li Jon is our son."

She saw hope flicker again in the woman's eyes, like the flame of a candle stirring in the wind. The woman reached out a hand to clutch Margaret's arm, and Margaret could feel the desperation in her bony grasp. "Then I beg you to help me, lady." She glanced at Li Jon. "You are a mother. I am a mother, too. But my little girl is gone."

ABOUT THE AUTHOR

RUPERT MORGAN has won various awards for his writing, including being a Young Writer of the Year for both *The Sunday Times* and *Elle*. He has published a series of satirical novels that have been translated in numerous languages (published in France by Éditions Belfond and Éditions 10/18), including *Let There Be Lite* and *Something Sacred*. For many years now he has lived in France, dividing his time between fiction and working as a cinema critic.

***The Consultant* on www.paperplanes.fr:**

- an audio version read by Saul Jephcott
- Rupert Morgan talks about writing *The Consultant*